GOSPEL CENTERED
CHURCH

Becoming the Community God Wants You to Be

Steve Timmis and Tim Chester

Gospel-Centered Church
© 2002 Steve Timmis and Tim Chester/The Good Book Company
All rights reserved. Reprinted with revisions 2003, 2005, 2007, 2009, 2012.
This US edition published 2017. Reprinted 2018.

This book first appeared as a series of articles in the UK edition of *The Briefing*.

The Good Book Company
Tel: 866 244 2165
Email: admin@thegoodbook.com

Websites:
UK: www.thegoodbook.co.uk
N America: www.thegoodbook.com
Australia: www.thegoodbook.com.au
New Zealand: www.thegoodbook.co.nz

Scripture quotations are from The Holy Bible, English Standard Version, copyright © 2001 by
Crossway Bibles, a division of Good News Publisher

ISBN: 978-1-90556-429-3

Cover design: Steve Devane
Printed in Turkey

CONTENTS

INTRODUCTION

When the Bible talks about the church—the people of God—it uses a variety of exciting and dynamic images. We are the bride yearning for our wedding day and beautifying ourselves for it. We are a thriving, bustling city of people drawn from every race and walk of life. We are the active body, directed and controlled by Jesus Christ our Head. We are the pilgrim people of God, being led across the desert to the promised land. We are the army of the Lord, wielding the sword of the Spirit, which is the word of God. We are the light on a hill, shining the hope of salvation to a lost world.

But ask an impartial observer to come up with a metaphor for what he observes in most churches today, and we would get a very different set of images: we are fossils, hidden away in our museum-piece buildings. We are tortoises, who move so slowly because we are inherently conservative and resistant to change. We are a spluttering candle that gives little light to anyone or anything. We are a cozy club, dedicated to the preservation of our curious rituals, outdated music, archaic buildings and stubborn and unreactive structures.

To greater or lesser degrees, many churches have fallen into the trap of accepting and perpetuating their own "evangelical" traditions, and have failed to remain dynamic, active and open to change for the gospel's sake. The result has been painfully obvious. A great decline in those involved in church, and many congregations that have, for whatever reason, simply lost their way.

In recent years, we have been bombarded with prescriptions for shaking our churches out of this deadly spiral. We have been encouraged to adopt new styles of worship, new cell or small-group structures, alternative leadership patterns or the principles of business re-engineering. While there is value in many of these approaches and techniques, they are ultimately doomed to failure if they do not spring from the nature of the gospel truths which we are both saved by and serve.

This book is an attempt at being truly "radical" about our understanding of church. Our aim has been to go back to our roots—the gospel—and see what kind of community it should create.

The principles this book explores are, therefore, an attempt to "nail down" what a gospel-centered church should look like in practice.

By "gospel-centered church" we mean more than simply a group of people that engage in evangelism. We mean a church in which the whole of its life and activities are shaped by the content and imperatives of the gospel.

We want to identify certain key features of such a church so that it is possible to measure the extent to which we are being faithful to our Master and His message. They are principles that can be worked out in a range of situations and they are as applicable to those in a traditional or established church as they are to those involved in a new venture.

These principles are not confined to those involved in "professional" ministry. They are, rather, an attempt at creating the outlines of a *gospel culture* for the whole church. Because of this, they should not be seen as the final word on the matter, or an exhaustive list.

It is our hope that this workbook will be used prayerfully by individuals, groups, church councils, elderships and study groups, with the aim that we start to think more biblically and seriously about how we can make our congregations more clearly gospel-centered. It is only by this practical obedience to the word of God, which leaves behind the traditions of men, that we can build healthy churches in our land.

Nor are these principles a prescription for results. Sorry to say, they do not come with a guarantee that converts will roll off the production line, or from our own wonderful experiences of success. Gospel ministry is hard work and gospel success is often difficult to measure. That is because conversion is the work of God. It is only the Spirit of life who can give life. This is a great truth and as the people of God we should glory in it.

But does that let us off the hook? Does this mean that our work cannot be assessed? Certainly not. We should assess what we are doing. We should ask hard questions of one another's ministry. But we must make sure they are the right questions...

Steve Timmis and Tim Chester

Finding your way around

 ### Consider this

A scenario—often based on a real-life situation—which raises some kind of dilemma or frustration in gospel ministry.

 ### Biblical background

A relevant Bible passage together with some questions to help you think it through.

 ### Read all about it

A discussion of the principle, both in terms of its theological underpinning and its contemporary application.

 ### Questions for discussion

Questions that can be used for group discussion or personal reflection.

 ### Ideas for action

Some ideas or an exercise to help people think through the application of the principle to their own situation.

We have tried to make this book work:

- whether it is read by an individual or used as the basis for group discussion.

- whether you want to work through it systematically or turn to particular topics as they arise in church life.

PART ONE

THE PRIORITY OF MISSION

1 MISSION AT THE CENTER

Mission is the central purpose of the church in the world.

Consider this

The Church Council of St Bartholomew's are meeting on a cold November night. Or maybe it is the quarterly church meeting of Springfield Evangelical Church. What is going to be on the agenda tonight? There will be an update from the pastoral committee, the treasurer's report, a discussion on the refurbishment of the ladies' "facilities", and who should speak at the church weekend. But the big item is the discussion on whether to buy a new songbook. No doubt these are all matters that need the attention of someone in the church. But is this what church is really about? What should be the focus of our attention when we make our plans?

Biblical background

Read Acts 1 v 6-11

- ❓ Why did Jesus leave the disciples when He ascended into heaven?

- ❓ Where does mission begin and where does it end according to v 8? *When the HS comes (begins) gives power and they will be witnesses*

- ❓ What is the purpose of the Holy Spirit according to v 8? *To give power. to the ends of the earth*

- ❓ What is the link between the ascension of Jesus and the mission He gives to us (see Matthew 28 v 18-20)?

Read all about it

This first principle of gospel ministry hardly needs any explanation or defense: "mission is the central purpose of the church in the world". Mission—telling others the good news of Jesus—is Christ's command to His church. Acts 1 reminds us that Jesus left His followers on earth to continue what He had begun, equipping them by the Spirit to be His witnesses. Mission reflects the love of God and it is the only hope for a world ruined by sin and facing God's eternal judgment. Above all, God is glorified as Christ is proclaimed and people submit to Him.

And a vision for mission must be a vision for the nations. God's purpose is to gather men and women from every nation. The gospel is for the world. We are the losers if we deprive ourselves of the excitement of what God is doing around the world and the resulting richness of Christian experience.

Who will argue that mission is not the purpose of the church? As Emil Brunner famously said: "The church exists by mission as a fire exists by burning".

The problem is the gap between our rhetoric and the reality of our practice. A friend of mine, who was converted in his twenties, looked forward with great eagerness to his first church business meeting. This was when the church would plot the downfall of Satan. Or so he assumed. The reality was a huge disappointment. The time was spent discussing which type of paper to buy in for the toilets.

Someone was telling me recently about the difficulties she faced as a Brit fitting into American culture. One of her struggles was with people who said: "Let's do lunch sometime". She expected them to phone and arrange a date—they never did. "Let's do lunch" was just an idiomatic way of saying farewell. It carried all the conviction of a Brit saying: "How are you?" We all say: "Let's do mission," but does it carry any more intent than: "Let's do lunch"?

The key word in this principle is "central", whereas we have made mission "peripheral". For most of us, and most of our churches, mission is one thing we do among others. And so, for example, we have a mission team alongside a pastoral team, a home-group team, a team that deals with the building, a youth team and a music team.

People are beginning to say we need "missionary theology" rather than "a theology of mission". Mission can no longer be looked at as one branch of theology. All theology must be missionary in its orientation.

We need the same reorientation as churches. We are in a missionary situation (as indeed we always have been). So all that we do must be missionary. That does not mean the only thing a church should do is proclaim the gospel to unbelievers. But it does mean our teaching, training, prayer, pastoral care, youth work, praise and so on must all contribute to the mission of the church.

There is great rejoicing in heaven over every sinner who is brought back to God. And we have all tasted something of that joy when we have known people converted. Of course mission involves disappointment and sacrifice. But there is no greater excitement than seeing Christ glorified before our eyes as men and women submit to Him. What else is worth putting at the center of your life?

Questions for discussion

- ❓ Describe the missionary situation in which you are placed.

- ❓ What does it mean for mission to be the priority in church life?

- ❓ What do you think is the most important reason for giving priority to mission?

- ❓ Is your church focused on mission or maintenance?

- ❓ What might it mean in practice to make *"your teaching, training, prayer, pastoral care, youth work, praise … contribute to the mission of the church"*?

Ideas for action

Imagine you are part of a church planting team in, say, Spain. Discuss your answers to the following questions with someone else, perhaps with your Bible-study group, and write down your answers.

❓ What criteria would you use to decide where to live?

❓ How would you approach secular employment?

❓ What standard of living would you expect as pioneer missionaries?

❓ What would you spend your time doing?

❓ What opportunities would you be looking for?

❓ What would your prayers be like?

❓ What would you be trying to do with your new friends?

❓ What kind of team would you want around you?

❓ How would you conduct your meetings together?

We find it easier to be radical in our thinking when we transplant ourselves outside our current situation, but you are as much a missionary here and now as you would be were you part of that team in Spain. Mission is the central purpose for us wherever we are. Check whether your answers describe your life now.

In his book, *Mission Minded* [Matthias Media, 1992], Peter Bolt encourages churches to draw a grid with the activities of the church down one side and across the top different stages in the process of preparing for mission: raising awareness, sharing the gospel and follow-up. This allows churches to check how each activity contributes to mission and to look for the gaps.

2 MISSION FOR EVERYONE

All believers are witnesses to the
good news of Jesus Christ.

Consider this

The train was pulling out of the station and Robert sat
looking at the couple sitting opposite him. He knew
they were going all the way to London, and that meant they had
about three hours "together". He smiled and they both gave him a
reluctant acknowledgment.

"Oh no," he thought to himself. "What on earth am I going to
say?" He decided to carry on reading his newspaper or at least look
as if he was. It soon became obvious they were not going to strike
up a conversation, but he knew he just had to.

At least, that is what the visiting preacher had said the night
before. He had made it sound all so easy—and so exciting. Robert
really did want to talk to them, and explain the gospel to them; after
all, it might be the only chance they had of hearing it. The weight of
their eternal destiny pressed down on him and he tried desperately
to think of a way in. Maybe he should offer to get them something
from the buffet car? But as he looked at them, his resolve quickly
evaporated.

In what seemed no time at all Robert heard the voice of the train
manager informing passengers that the train was due to arrive at
their destination in under ten minutes. He just sank into his seat,
despairing at his inadequacy.

What should Robert have done? Was he right to try to talk to his fellow travelers? Was he wrong to have made such a big thing out of it?

Biblical background

Read 1 Peter 3 v 13-16

? Who initiates a gospel conversation in v 15 and why do they initiate it?

? What is the link between setting apart Christ as Lord in our hearts and being asked questions about the gospel?

? What kind of behavior will provoke questions from unbelievers (look back over 2 v 12 – 3 v 12)?

? What kind of preparation can we do to be ready to give the reason for our hope?

Read all about it

I have lost count of how many times I have heard the challenge to tell people about Jesus. And I have grown weary of the condemnation it inevitably brings because of my reluctance or inability. Even books that promise to make evangelism slightly less difficult tend to leave me groaning at my own inadequacies. Part of my problem is that I am not a natural extrovert. As a result I do not find talking to strangers easy. I am well known among my friends for my stilted attempts at social chatter. But I have stopped being so hard on myself. Popeye was right: "I yam what I yam"! I cannot be someone else and, significantly, God does not want me to try.

So does this let me off the hook? Yes! In the sense that I do not have to go through life gritting my teeth, clenching my fists and wiping the beads of sweat of my troubled brow as a prelude to forcing a gospel conversation with a complete stranger.

But it does not let me off the hook in the sense that God *does* want me to bear a credible witness to the gospel in whatever context I find myself. Many years ago my youth leader pointed out that, as a Christian, you cannot help but be a witness: the only question is what kind of witness. I have never forgotten those words.

We are not all gifted, eloquent, vivacious, engaging personal evangelists. But we **are** all children of God, saved by grace and heading for glory. Commending the One who has adopted, rescued and enriched us is an enormous privilege. This is the heart of the principle. The source of this consistent and believable witness is the sense of being awe-struck by grace. Gripped by grace to the extent that it infuses our hearts and transforms our lives. This grace will also nurture within us a love for those who, in the words of Jonah, have "forsaken the grace that could be theirs".

Loving God to the extent that we want to make His truth winsome, and loving others to the extent that we want them to know the God of truth is not the exclusive prerogative of preachers, evangelists and missionaries.

Paul concludes a significant section within 1 Corinthians with these words: "Be imitators of me, as I am of Christ" (1 Corinthians 11 v 1). What we are to imitate is disclosed in the section that runs from 8 v 1, and contains such searching phrases as:

- *though I am free from all, I have made myself a servant to all, that I might win more of them. (9 v 19)*
- *I have become all things to all people, that by all means I might save some. (9 v 22)*
- *I do it all for the sake of the gospel. (9 v 23)*
- *I try to please everyone in everything I do, not seeking my own advantage, but that of many, that they may be saved. (10 v 33)*

God in His providence has placed us all in a range of situations. Thankfully we are not all full-time Christian workers and, as a result, we rub shoulders with scores of non-Christians at the medical center and the school gates, in the classroom and staff room, board room and changing room, on the field and on the factory floor, driving the car and serving at the check-out. The list is almost endless, yet these are the contexts for our testimony to the saving power of the gospel. We do that through our actions and our attitudes, in our behavior and our relationships, by our ambitions and our motivation. We show the power of God through our gentleness and thoughtfulness, through our refusal to trample on others and undermine their credibility in our gossip. We respect everyone by virtue of who they are as God's image-bearers. We love and serve even those who despise and demean us.

Such behavior will surely give us opportunity to explain the good news that is Jesus, but as the saying goes: *"If they'll listen, tell them; if they won't, show them"*. It is a win-win situation, but only because it is all about seeing God glorified through people being saved.

One of the virtues of these principles of gospel ministry is that they open up involvement in gospel work. Every Christian without exception is called to be a minister of the gospel and to live their lives for the gospel. This is what is so liberating about this particular principle. It releases us *into* the task of making Jesus known in whatever circumstances we find ourselves. It sets before us the immense privilege of making a significant contribution to the evangelism process. Our lives, and even our stumbling words, all play a part in realizing the purposes of God in the lives of the people with whom we have contact. Which means that although I may remain silent for the whole of my train journey to London, Mrs Patel at the corner shop is going to come face to face with authentic Christianity on a daily basis.

Questions for discussion

? Have you ever shared Robert's sense of frustration?

? If it is true that you cannot help but be a witness, what kind of a witness are you?

? Think about the contexts in which you "rub shoulders" with unbelievers. What is the distinctive gospel behavior that should characterize your relationships?

? How can you encourage, or "set free", the timid in your congregation to be witnesses for Christ?

? Jim Wallis writes: "Evangelism in our day has largely become a packaged production, a mass-marketed experience in which evangelists strain to answer that question which nobody is asking ... When the life of the church no longer raises any questions, evangelism degenerates." Can you see any evidence for this claim?

Ideas for action

The gospel should change our worldview, affecting how we approach any issue. This means that every topic has the potential to be a gospel opportunity. In your church or Bible-study group provide a regular slot in which someone presents a Christian perspective on a current news item or reviews a book or film. And when you talk together—even if it is just catching up on the events of the day—encourage people to apply gospel principles to the subject of conversation.

3 MISSION AND WORSHIP

Principle

Worship is about the whole of life
rather than just meetings.

Consider this

Here we are, gathered on a cold night in the warmth of
our church building. The old wood and gleaming brass
seem strangely reassuring. The leading of the meeting has been
as polished as always. Now the music group are giving an accomplished performance as they introduce us to a great new song.
Then, suddenly, in bursts Amos, a notorious farmhand, scruffy
and unkempt. As he is ushered out by the stewards, you hear him
shouting:

> "Away with the noise of your songs!
> I will not listen to the music of your harps.
> But let justice roll on like a river,
> righteousness like a never-failing stream."
> (Amos 5 v 23-24)

Okay, so Amos is not going to turn up next Sunday evening. But
what resonance do his words have for us today?

Biblical background

Read Romans 11 v 33–12 v 2

? What is the cause of Paul's praise in 11 v 33-36?

? What is a living sacrifice?

? How are we to be transformed?

? How does this qualify as worship?

Read all about it

Worship has been a frequent point of discussion, even conflict, in recent years. It was a common theme, too, for the Old Testament prophets. In Isaiah 58 the people of Israel complain that God does not hear them. The prophets are quick to attack attempts to manipulate God through religious performance. But here the people "seem eager" for God to come near them (v 2). This is not mere religious duty. Their worship seems genuine and their intent earnest. They want to know God. They want to be near Him. And yet He still remains distant.

The problem is that their worship is divorced from the rest of their lives (v 3-5). Even as they fast and pray, they exploit their workers. We cannot separate commitment to God from commitment to other people. What kind of worship is God looking for? It is to work for social justice, to oppose oppression, to care for the poor (v 6-7). Love for God is expressed as love for our neighbors.

Singing pleases God when it expresses a grateful heart, a reverent fear and a life offered in submission. But we must not mistake the form for the substance. Singing itself is not the point. Indeed singing detached from a life of submission is abhorrent to God. *Good music does not mean good worship.*

In Isaiah 12 Isaiah calls upon the people to "give thanks" and "sing to the Lord, for he has done glorious things". But this is not a call to gather in the temple. It is a call to mission. It is "among the nations" that we are to "proclaim that his name is exalted". The world will not hear if we sing in "worship services" in our church buildings. The greatest worship we can offer God is to gather more worshippers. It is striking that in the chapter of the New Testament that speaks most of congregational gatherings—1 Corinthians 14—the one person who is said to worship is the new convert who turns to Christ.

What does this mean? It means the goal of our meetings should be to encourage one another to worship God—not just then and there, but throughout the week. We meet to "stir up one another to love and good works" (Hebrews 10 v 24). That is the criterion by which to judge all contributions to our gatherings. Even our corporate singing is to be judged by this criterion (Colossians 3 v 16). And the job of the person leading the meeting is to provide a framework in which we can exhort *one another* to serve God and proclaim His glory to the nations.

Many accept that the New Testament does not speak of the early Christians meeting to "worship" God, but rather to encourage and exhort one another; that worship in the New Testament is about a life lived in the service of God, not about singing or liturgy. And yet still we make a big deal of the "worship service". Our churches teach that worship is a "life thing", but we put our energies into the meeting—into putting on a good show. Our meetings are the focus of church life when surely it should be our mission that is the focus of church life. Our church "service" should not describe a meeting, but the offer of the gospel to the community around us.

It is not that worship is unimportant. Rather, it is so important that we should do it all the time. So worthy is our God that He deserves the worship of lives lived in obedience to Him all day and every day. So great is His mercy that we should offer our bodies as living sacrifices—this is our spiritual worship (Romans 12 v 1).

How does this look

21

Questions for discussion

? What is wrong with talking about "a time of worship"?

? What is the link between worship and mission?

? How can we encourage people to think of worship as something you do on Monday morning?

Ideas for action

List the things you did last time you met as a church or Bible-study group, from the time you first arrived to the time you left. How do they measure up against the criterion of enabling us to "stir up one another to love and good works".

? How could they be changed to better fulfil this end?

4 | MISSION OUTSIDE OUR COMFORT ZONE

Principle

The gospel drives us out of our cozy, safe comfort zone.

Consider this

Fred had been developing a friendship with George at the office for some months. Several times he had invited him to church, but George had always declined. It wasn't his thing. Fred didn't know what to do next. He wanted George to become a Christian, but George wasn't interested in church. Now George had invited him to go to the greyhound track with him. What should he do? He wasn't sure what his friends at church thought about greyhound racing. For that matter, he wasn't sure what he thought about it.

Biblical background

Read Luke 14 v 7-24

❓ Who does Jesus instruct us to invite into our homes and why?

❓ Why does Jesus tell the story of the banquet in v 16-24?

❓ Who are the "poor, crippled, blind and lame" in our society?

Read all about it

You might like to try it. I asked the members of my church to go into a betting shop and place a bet on a horse before the next meeting. There was (I am glad to say) uproar. "Trust me," I said. "I don't want to encourage gambling, but trust me—all will be explained next week."

About half of them did it—myself included. The following week I asked people what it felt like. This is a selection of our replies:

- It was an alien environment.
- I hadn't got a clue what to do.
- It was better with a friend.
- I felt very awkward, nervous, very odd and on edge.
- I felt that people were looking at me.
- No one talked to me—and I was glad about that.
- I wanted to get in and out as quickly as possible.
- The people inside were very different from me.

The excuses of those who did not do it were just as revealing:

- I don't agree with it.
- I didn't want to be seen.
- I didn't want to be misinterpreted.
- I couldn't be bothered.
- I was brought up a Methodist.
- I wouldn't know what to do.
- I would be excruciatingly embarrassed.
- I wouldn't like the people in there.

This, I suggest, is how most people today feel about going to church. It brings home to us what an unrealistic expectation it is to ask many people (admittedly, not all) to come to church.

But it also highlights how cut off from our culture we can be and how unaware of this we often are. A lot of evangelism revolves around getting people to come to church or church events. For some this is appropriate, but most people are no more likely to enter a church than you or I are to go into a betting shop. Many people no longer even go to church for rites of passage.

Church is where we feel safe and comfortable. Church is where non-Christians feel embarrassed and awkward. We offer people the gospel, but on our terms and on our territory. Put like this, it becomes clear that we must take the gospel—and indeed the church—out of our comfort zone and into the world around us.

And this is becoming clearer. A generation ago there were suffi-cient "religious", God-fearing people to make a church-building-based ministry viable. And some churches still flourish on this basis. But even the largest of these churches are failing to reach perhaps two-thirds of their communities.

Even friendship evangelism, where the emphasis is on sharing the gospel in the context of friendship rather than the context of a church event, can keep us in our comfort zone. We end up reaching people who are like us—our friends. Almost by definition, friend-ship evangelism leaves the socially marginalised untouched. And yet these were precisely the people Jesus went out of His way to include. But it is not just among the socially marginalised that we do not always feel safe. For some, stepping out of our comfort zone may mean engaging in a gospel way with academia, politics, business or the media.

It would be great to see some of our "successful" churches planting congregations into homes and community centers in the estates and communities that are untouched by the gospel; to see more Christians getting involved in the residents' association, the advice center, the local playgroup and so on. We can support those who stand for the gospel in public life or in their profession rather than burden them with ecclesiastical responsibilities. And why not strip away some of those meetings—"down-size" church—to give Christians more time to spend out of our comfort zone?

In Luke 14 Jesus is invited to a party where He observes people jostling for places of honor. He says our parties should not be like that. Nor should we invite only those who will return the invitation. Instead, we should invite "the poor, the crippled, the lame, the blind" (v 13). Why? Because God—the Master of the great eternal party—has thrown open His banquet to "the poor, the crippled, the blind and the lame" (v 21). Jesus urges us out of our comfort zone in imitation of our gracious Father. He himself left the splendor and security of heaven to live—and die—among us. And, just as the Father sent Him, so He now sends us (John 20 v 21).

Questions for discussion

? How do you think your non-Christian friends would feel about going to church?

? Are there communities in your area that are not being reached with the gospel because your focus is on friendship evangelism or because you are fearful of leaving your comfort zone?

? Are there Christians in your church who are engaging in a gospel way in specialist areas: academia, politics, business or the media? How could you support them?

Ideas for action

Think about the places where your non-Christian contacts feel most comfortable. How can you take the gospel and the church to these places? Some churches have held meetings in public function rooms; others have hired a hotel. One church ran the pub quiz one night a week, giving them the platform to hold a simple carol service in the pub. Another church had an "evangelistic program" one autumn which involved encouraging—and goading—one another to join a local club or do voluntary work in the community. And why not try placing a bet on a horse—just to see what it feels like.

5 MISSION WITHOUT COMPROMISE

Principle

Gospel ministry is contemporary, daring and biblical.

Consider this

The church business meeting promised to be a stormy affair. Word had got out that two of the church leaders were absent last Sunday evening from the evangelistic guest service because they had gone to the local jazz club. Understandably, some of the church members were appalled. It was now public knowledge and some people were asking for the leaders to step down because they were no longer fit to lead the church. In the case of one of them, this would mean effectively giving him the sack because the church employed him. After an opening prayer, and a word of explanation, the two leaders were asked to explain themselves. The leaders had gone with two members from the church and four non-Christians and the purpose was to build a friendship with these people. They would never have attended the guest service, and jazz was a common interest. Some other people spoke up and commented on the inappropriateness of going to such a place, going on a Sunday and missing meeting with other believers.

Biblical background

Read Philippians 1 v 12-30

? Why does Paul rejoice in his imprisonment (v 12-20)?

? What does Paul live for (v 21-26)?

? What should be the central criterion that determines the conduct of the Philippians (v 27)? How might you express this as a question that could be applied to your decision making?

? How does the gospel shape our response to opposition, suffering and struggle (v 28-30)?

Read all about it

Sometimes I like to just sit and think about the gospel and it never ceases to amaze me. The God who made the universe, who is holy and awesome, sovereign and omnipotent, patiently and deliberately deals with the human race, and has led all history to the point where He became a fertilized egg in the womb of a young virgin! It really is mind-blowing. Yet think how the story unfolds. He grows inside the womb, is born in less than auspicious circumstances and lives as part of an ordinary, everyday kind of family. He's 30 years old before He begins what turns out to be a rather short public ministry. During which He meets Satan in a head-to-head, spends His time with a reluctant band of disciples, deals with religious bigots, and ends up being abused by a group of soldiers. He's finally hung up as a public spectacle on an instrument of torture, and under the cloak of darkness, experiences hell itself as He hangs in isolation under the judgment of God.

From throne to manger, from palace to slums, from heaven to hell: how daring and radical is that? We worship a God who undertook an arduous, costly, demanding, and we might even say risky, rescue mission to set us free and make us His own.

How is it then that we who believe in this incredible God are so prone to caution when it comes to gospel ministry? We are most comfortable when we're treading well-worn paths, like designating the Sunday evening service as evangelistic, holding open air meetings or running evangelistic courses. Of course these are good things, but we should also think about the people we're *not* reaching by these initiatives. It's at this point we need to engage in some serious biblical reflection that prompts and equips us for contemporary, daring and radical ministry.

In one UK city of some 600,000 there are almost certainly less than 10,000 evangelicals. If each believer is reaching 10 people with the gospel (a generous estimate!), it still leaves half a million people unreached. And what about the world? It's estimated that a staggering 1.3 billion still haven't heard the gospel. We do have a responsibility for these, don't we? For the thousands upon thousands in our towns and cities, and the billion or so in our world?

If so, then nothing less than contemporary, daring and radical ministry will do in order to make any impact. This will mean a willingness to leave the paths we know so well and move out of our familiar environments. It will probably mean responding in kind to the heart of a God who was willing to undertake an arduous, demanding and costly rescue mission on our behalf.

What might this look like? That will depend on local circumstances, but here are four examples.

1. A local church has responded to the opening of a shopping center next to them by moving their Sunday morning service and running a children's club for kids of parents who come Christmas shopping.

2. One church decided that for every pound it spent on internal ministry—on hymn books, minister's salary and so on—it would spend an equal amount on mission.

3. A group of Christians wanted to reach the people in a notorious

area, and so bought a couple of houses, and moved people in to live and work there.

4. Some others bought a pub and a launderette on a housing estate and ran them for the local community, while also using the pub as a venue for their Sunday meetings.

For some, these may not look that daring, but for others they will be "off the wall"! We're not so naïve as to think they will be greeted with a sudden rush of enthusiasm and response. You may not like what they've done, and you may not agree with their decisions, but on what grounds could any of these examples be *legitimately* criticized?

Examples 1 and 4 raise issues such as what Christians do with Sunday, and how Christians view pubs. There are some people who would rule these out because:

⊟ they violate the idea of Sunday as a day that's holy and set apart for the Lord.

⊟ pubs and alcohol are not things with which Christians should be associated.

These concerns need to be addressed. We must not compromise on being biblical. Gospel ministry must arise out of careful and humble theological reflection. It is important that we don't fall prey to mere pragmatism. So let's engage in some reflection...

Even if we concede Sunday as a special day, how does the activity of the Christians in the examples above violate that? These people are about gospel work—deliberately and self-consciously. They are engaged in activities that enable them to get alongside and reach non-Christians. That is the motivation and that seems to be a great activity for "the Lord's Day".

As for pubs, it cannot be insignificant that Jesus spent time with the riff-raff of Jewish society, the outcasts and the nobodies. The religious people criticized Him and accused Him of being a glutton and a drunkard, yet most evangelicals I know never come close to such an accusation being levelled at them. Jesus didn't associate with the rejects simply because He liked a good meal and enjoyed a sip of wine. He did it because He wanted to win them. He wanted to find the lost and bring them home. He wanted to be the physician of souls to those that knew they were sick. Which, in the light of the truths rehearsed at the beginning of this chapter, should not surprise us.

Questions for discussion

? Is your church more likely to fall into the trap of unprincipled pragmatism or ineffectual idealism?

? Would you describe Paul's ministry as contemporary, daring and radical or as arising out of biblical and theological reflection? Why in many churches are these categories mutually exclusive?

? What stops you being daring for the gospel?

Ideas for action

Spend the next month:

⬎ Looking around your community.

⬎ Thinking about your church program.

⬎ Analysing the approach of Jesus and the apostles to reaching people.

⬎ Talking through your evangelistic strategy.

⬎ Asking God to intensify your concern for His glory and the conversion of sinners.

Then decide on one new initiative that is demanding and a departure from "the norm". You do not need everyone in church involved in the activity itself, but you do need everyone informed about it and praying for it. Then go for it. If it fails, learn from it. If it succeeds, praise God for it. But at the very least people will have heard the gospel and you will have risked something for the sake of the gospel. Which places you in rather good company.

6 MISSION WITHOUT FEAR

Principle

It is better to take gospel initiatives that fail than to fail to take gospel initiatives.

Consider this

Peter trudged home after the meeting, head down, hands deep in his pockets. It had seemed such a great idea—a drop-in café for the young people who regularly hung around the church building. It would give them an alternative to the streets and lead to gospel opportunities. He had imagined holding Bible studies, planning weekends away, discipleship courses. But for the first few weeks no one had come except kids whose parents went to the church. Then a group had come together just to be disruptive. A window had been broken and some money stolen. Now the church leaders had called a halt. Secretly Peter was relieved. Next time he had a big idea, he would keep his big mouth shut.

Biblical background

Read Matthew 25 v 14-30

❓ Which of the three servants does the master describe as "good and faithful" and why?

❓ Why did the third servant not use what the master had given him?

❓ How does our view of God affect our behavior?

Read all about it

Nobody likes to fail. Nobody wants to be left looking stupid by an evangelistic initiative that badly missed the mark. Nobody wants to be bruised by a church planting project that fell apart. But the fear of failure can be a significant impediment to the work of the gospel. Someone suggests a new gospel initiative and we immediately think of ten reasons why it might not work. The result is inertia.

This principle does not mean we should be rash. There is no virtue in being foolish. Nor does it mean we should not ask questions about what will work and what will not work. We want to be effective in gospel ministry. We want to use our resources wisely. It does mean we should be ready to try new ideas. And it means we should be ready to stop them if they do not work. There should be no embarrassment about trying something and then saying: "Well that clearly didn't work. What are we going to try next?" We probably learn as much through failure as we do through success.

I remember sitting on a bus, converted into a mobile Christian resource center, replete with gospel literature, videos, posters, refreshments and not an unbeliever in sight. Would I do it again? No way. Do I regret doing it? Not at all. We tried. We failed. But that is better than doing nothing. And in the meantime, God blessed us as a church. We saw people saved in ways we could never have imagined, let alone planned.

And what is lost if we fail? It may be the reputation of the gospel and that is something about which we should be rightly concerned and rightly cautious. But more often than not all that is really at stake is our reputation. The issue is not just our willingness to try new things for the gospel. The issue is our definitions of success. If we measure success in terms of our reputation with our peers, the numbers in our congregation or the professionalism of our Sunday meetings, then we are going to be "risk-averse". But if "success" is to be faithful to the gospel, then we will be, we must be, creative for the sake of the gospel.

The whole issue is brought into sharp focus if we use the term "sin" instead of the term "failure". Is it a sin to try something for the sake of gospel that does not work? If I speak to a friend about Christ and they are not converted, have I sinned? Of course not. But if I do not offer hope to those who are without hope, if I do not speak the word of life to those who are dying, is that a sin? Yes it is. The servant in Jesus' parable who buried his talent in the ground is described by the master as a "wicked, lazy servant" and is thrown outside into the darkness (Matthew 25 v 14-30).

In Ezekiel 33 God describes how, if a watchman sounds the warning of impending peril, the people are responsible for their own fate. But if the watchman fails to sound the warning, the watchman shares responsibility for the fate of the people. You can almost imagine the criminal injury court determining the watchman's culpability. Did he sound the warning or not? In the same way, says God, if Ezekiel does not warn of God's judgment, he shares responsibility for the fate of the people. But if he does warn, the people will be responsible for their own fate. If we sound the gospel warning and people do not respond, then we will be heart-broken. We may have egg on our faces. Our reputation may plummet. But that is better than failing to sound the warning or sounding it so cautiously that no one can hear.

Questions for discussion

[?] How does the Bible define "failure"?

[?] Can you think of evangelistic ideas you have been involved in which "failed"? Was it right to have tried them?

[?] It is great to have a mixture of cautious people and risk-takers. Which are you? How can you help ensure the church takes radical gospel initiatives without being foolish or wasteful?

Ideas for action

Next time you think of ten ready reasons *not to do* something, make sure you consider ten reasons *to do* it before dismissing the idea completely.

In my previous church we changed the pattern of our meetings together—the when, where and what—seven or eight times in as many years. Maybe we were fickle; maybe we were too stupid to get it right first time—or seventh time. But I think we were constantly adapting to changing circumstances. How good is your church at stopping activities that no longer work well? Are there any current activities that need reviewing?

In our church plenty of people have had a go at leading a meeting or giving a Bible study. We have given some training to each of them. Some have not been up to it. We have had to say: "This is not for you. Let's think together what your gift is." With one or two this has been quite painful, especially when they have associated "ministry" primarily with preaching and leading meetings. Others have flourished and are now leading groups and heading up gospel initiatives.

▣ Identify the people in your church or Bible-study group who might be given the opportunity to lead a meeting, take a Bible study, mentor a younger Christian or lead an evangelistic initiative. Can you think of contexts in which they can "have a go"?

PART TWO

THE PRIORITY OF PEOPLE

7 THE PRIORITY OF PEOPLE

Church exists wherever believers are covenanted together under the authority of the word of God.

Consider this

Two Christian families and a single Christian live in the small village of Puddleduck. There is no evangelical church in the village so they all attend churches a few miles away in the local town. They have good contacts with their neighbors and often have opportunities to share the gospel. They would love to start a gospel work in the village. But first they need to find a building, a minister, some finance and someone to play an instrument, not to mention the daunting process of agreeing a constitution. *Or do they?*

Biblical background

Read Acts 2 v 42-47

? What features of church life in Jerusalem does Luke highlight in v 42?

? Why do you think he regards these as important?

? Do these have a continuing relevance for a local church?

? Is anything else necessary to be a "real" church?

Read all about it

This principle may appear out of place among principles designed to "nail down" what a gospel ministry means in practice and a means of creating a gospel culture. At first glance it appears rather academic and theoretical. But nothing could be further from the truth. Our understanding of church and what we mean when we use that word is of enormous gospel consequence.

Church is one of those evocative words that conjures up rich images. Usually those involve gothic buildings, loud bells, the heady smell of wood polish, and, all too frequently, public appeals for the roof fund. Those images may not necessarily spring to the mind of good evangelicals, but we have our own sub-conscious images. These include a mixture of tangibles and intangibles: buildings, pulpits, constitutions, staff, membership, communion tables, deacons, councils, written orders of service, musical instruments and so on. Are these essential to what it means to be church? How many of them are present in Luke's description of the early church in, for example, Acts 2?

The Greek word for church, *ecclesia*, was a common term in the first century and referred to a gathering of people, usually political in nature. It is used in Acts 19 v 32 to describe the angry crowd convened by Demetrius the silversmith, anxious about his income and the honor of the goddess Artemis. Few versions use the word "church" in their translation of *ecclesia* at that point, yet do so when they come across the word again in Acts 20 v 17. The reason seems obvious enough: the word "church" has become a specialized and overtly religious term and it seems improper to use it for a potentially riotous mob. But in the first century it was a term in common use that was deemed appropriate to describe a group of Christians when they met together. And that is the significant point: when they met together. The term is used (with the one possible exception of Acts 19 v 32) to describe a number of Christians in the act of gathering. The same word *ecclesia* is used in the Septuagint (the Greek version of the Old Testament) to describe the occasion when Israel gathered at Mount Sinai to receive the Law from Moses (Deuteronomy 9 v 10).

These observations inform an understanding of church that is both precise and shockingly minimalist.

The precision is important because it identifies that which really is essential. To be church (as distinct from any gathering of individuals with a common interest) it has to be people in relationship with God and each other who meet together. The purpose of that gathering, as it was for "the church" at Sinai, is to hear the word of God—the gospel—so that they might know how to live as God's covenant people.

Having a minimalist view of church like this is a great advantage in terms of gospel ministry. Church and mission are two sides of the same coin and "church" is God's mission strategy. As our first principle stated, the purpose of the church is mission. It is the task of the church as "a chosen race, a royal priesthood, a holy nation, a people for God's own possession" to declare the praises of "him who called you out of darkness into his marvellous light" (1 Peter 2 v 9). Church planting is a gospel strategy. An effective way to make inroads for the gospel in a locality is to plant a church there. But if we bury church under a barrow-load of incidentals such as buildings, clergy, hymn books, constitutions or whatever, then it becomes prohibitive in terms of time, money and personnel. The net result is the loss of a gospel opportunity.

Those involved in one church-planting initiative were identifying the most effective way forward and agreed to plant a church in an inner-city area. There were already three families living there and so all that was needed was for a number of Christians to start meeting regularly together in one of their homes. These people did not meet as a Bible-study group, a mere sub-set of the "real" church. From the beginning they met as the church in that place, with all the privileges and responsibilities that belong to that status. In the people who comprised the church, they also had all the resources they needed to do the gospel work God was calling them to in the area. Jesus only uses the term "church" three times, two of them in Matthew 18. It is in this context that He promises His presence where two or three meet together in His name (Matthew 18 v 20).

Understanding church in this way helps create a gospel culture by opening up all sorts of opportunities for gospel initiatives that are not even considered if we insist on, or are influenced by, extra-biblical and un-biblical definitions.

Questions for discussion

❓ What images does the word "church" evoke for you?

❓ What are the people, things or activities that you need for a church to be a church?

❓ What does this leave out? What are the people, things or activities that you do not need for a church to be a church?

❓ Are there ways in which you could "downsize" your church to make it more focused on mission?

Ideas for action

Identify the "trappings of church life"—those things that are not necessary for church life—that are currently getting in the way of the mission of your church or your involvement in mission. Are there meetings in your church week that you could stop attending in order to spend more time with non-Christians?

8 PEOPLE IN RELATIONSHIPS

Principle

Effective gospel ministry is long-term, // low-key and relational.

Consider this

A Christian worked in an inner-city area for five years. It was hard and demanding. At the end of his time he was nearing exhaustion and burn-out. But he had played his part and stuck at it. He had worked where most people would not dream of working. And so no one argued with him when he said it was time to go. Shortly after he had left, someone was in the area talking with one of "the locals". My friend's name cropped up in the conversation and the man from the area responded: "What would he know? He wasn't here long enough for us to get to know him."

Biblical background

Read 1 Thessalonians 2 v 1-12

- What are the strategies that Paul has rejected (v 1-6)?
  no pretense but greed
  no flattery, not putting on a mask to cover up greed
- What were the two things that Paul shared with the Thessalonians (v 8)? Can you think of Christians—maybe including yourself—who only share one of these things?
  not looking for praise
- What were the characteristics of Paul's ministry among the Thessalonians (v 7-12)?

Read all about it

Success is an intoxicating thing. We all want it and we are all impressed by it. If it is a straight choice between listening to someone who teaches it and does it, and someone who teaches it, does it and has been successful in it, we go for the latter every time. Because success validates ideas. Popular church folklore goes something like this: you can argue with opinions, but you cannot argue with full pews.

This deference to success carries with it a number of dangers, not least the seduction by technique. Because we all admire achievers, we want to know how they have achieved. And invariably we expect a set of digestible points which we can take back with us and apply the following Sunday. The way people have latched on to both the Willow Creek model of seeker-friendly services and the pattern of cell church illustrate the prevalence of this mindset. But, whatever the merits or otherwise of these two approaches, neither can be reduced to a guaranteed three-step guide to success. Of course we rejoice in stories of gospel success, but we need to be wary of converting them into quick-fix solutions for every situation.

A moment's biblical reflection soon disillusions such naïveté and exposes it for the faithlessness it is. Gospel ministry is seldom glamorous. More often than not it is a head-down, nose-to-grindstone, hard slog (see 2 Corinthians 4 v 7-18; 2 Timothy 2 v 1-6).

This is no counsel of despair—this principle talks about effective gospel ministry. But it argues for a different approach to gospel ministry than that shaped by a preoccupation with success; an approach that tries to understand gospel ministry on its own terms rather than simply as a technique or a means to an end. This principle identifies three key features of such an approach.

Long-term

Credibility and integrity lie at the heart of gospel proclamation and such virtues can only be demonstrated over a long period of time. Thinking long-term is particularly important when working with many non-Christians. In most cases we are starting so far back in terms of their knowledge of basic Christian truths and yet have to deal with so much prejudice concerning the irrelevancy of Christian faith. I have such a friend. It took me almost three years before he was willing even to listen to an explanation of what I believed. Of course, I could have walked away and shaken the dust off my feet in a "holy huff". But as "the church" was largely responsible for his scepticism, the least I could do was stick around and earn the right for the gospel to get a hearing.

Low-key

Being low-key does not preclude the occasional major event that is advertised in the local press, but it does claim that the bedrock of gospel ministry is the work that is going on quietly, day-by-day in the course of events. People sometimes want to come to see the work in which we are involved. The request is perfectly reasonable, but the problem is that what they see when they come is so unspectacular and ordinary—maybe even boring. On the surface, it is just "normal" people getting on with the normal business of life, such as friendship, work and leisure. What makes it significant is the clear and unambiguous gospel intention of the routine. Whether it is helping out a friend, a day at the office or going to the cinema, there is a commitment to building relationships, modelling the Christian faith and talking about the gospel as a natural part of conversation.

Relational

Society is far more familiar now than it was even fifteen years ago. Everyone is on first-name terms. Even the anonymous voices in a telephone call center are keen to use your Christian name when you contact them to place an order, or even to make a complaint. Relationships matter. We may despair of the superficiality, but the fact is that contemporary people expect to get closer sooner. This should not be a problem to us because relationships are at the heart of the gospel. The dismantling of some cultural barriers actually provides us with the opportunity to get alongside people and build friendships with them for the sake of the gospel. It is a vulnerable position, but it is one from which we can demonstrate a real and tangible godliness, in which they observe our mistakes and witness the power of grace. In 1 Thessalonians 2 v 8 Paul describes how he shared not only the gospel with the Thessalonians, but his very life as well.

Allowing this principle to shape our ministry may require some radical readjustments. It may make the immediate a little less pressing, the razzmatazz a little less appealing and professional detachment a little less attractive. It honors the countless faithful Christians who will never make it to a conference platform. What it does is provide an approach to gospel ministry that gives no guarantees concerning the admiration of the public or our peers. But if we equate either of those with an effective ministry, we have already lost our way.

Questions for discussion

❓ Are you disappointed to hear that gospel ministry cannot be "reduced to a guaranteed three-step guide to success"? Or are you encouraged to realize that your experience is normal?

❓ In 2 Corinthians 4 v 7-18 Paul talks about power and weakness; life and death. What is the relationship between them?

❓ In what ways should non-Christians find our gospel ministry ordinary? In what ways should they find it extraordinary?

Ideas for action

"It is just 'normal' people getting on with the normal business of life, such as friendship, work and leisure. What makes it significant is the clear and unambiguous gospel intention of the routine." List "the normal business of life" in which you regularly engage. In each case think through what it might mean to bring a "gospel intention" to the routine.

9 PEOPLE IN PARTNERSHIP

Involvement in society is best done
with other Christians.

Consider this

Life has been difficult since losing your job. The money
you received was very generous, but the prospect of
a new job has been quite stressful. You don't want to go back
to working those long hours and being away so often, but what
else can you do? A friend phones you late one evening and tells
you about some jobs coming up at the new megastore opening a
couple of miles away. He suggests you and one other friend apply
together. You say he's crazy. He says, think about it. As you do,
you keep turning over in your mind his arguments. There would
certainly be a lot more time at home and a lot more opportunity to
get involved with the church. But it's his final comment that really
gets you thinking: "If the three of us could work together, think
what opportunities it would give for the gospel. We could really
support and encourage each other, and help one another out when
it comes to explaining something. It would make the inevitable
social occasions a lot more bearable and productive as well." As
you drift into sleep your mind turns over what your old colleagues
would say: "From software to soap powder, what a career move!"

Biblical background

Read Acts 15 v 36 – 16 v 6

❓ What was the issue that caused Paul and Barnabas to part company? Why was it so important to them? How did they resolve the issue?

❓ Scan over Acts 13 – 15 and notice how often Luke refers to Paul and Barnabas together. Scan over Acts 16 – 17 and notice how often Luke refers to Paul and Silas together. What do you think is the significance of this?

❓ What do you think were the main reasons Paul chose to do mission as part of a team?

Read all about it

I guess the recurring message of these principles of gospel ministry is essentially "get out there and get on with it". But how do we best do that? As Principle No. 6 suggests, we should not allow the fear of failure to paralyze us—too much is at stake. But neither should we be foolish and irresponsible. That can sometimes happen. You listen to a stirring message or return from an inspiring conference and you are all wound up and raring to go. Unfortunately, no one else was stirred by the message or went to the conference. But that isn't going to stop you! You have often noticed the gang of skateboarders who congregate outside the cinema and you feel compelled to go and tell them about Jesus. Or it could be the homeless people who sleep under the railway bridge; or the prostitutes on the other side of town; or the bikers who meet by the roadside cafe; or the clubbers; the druggies; the golfers; the cleaning staff—the list of candidates is endless. Who or where they are is not the issue: your zeal to reach them is.

First, this principle offers a word of caution and restraint. In the early eighties I used to enjoy watching the US police drama *Hill*

Street Blues. Maybe it was my age or maybe it is my memory, but I remember it being compelling viewing. Part of each program would focus on the daily briefing sessions. They always ended with the duty sergeant reminding the detectives and officers as they made their way onto the streets: "Don't forget! It's dangerous out there". In the course of a series, however, there would be a police officer who forgot those words. He or she would become blasé, a little too familiar and comfortable, a little too "at home" with the dirt and grime. Predictably it would always end in a tragedy of corruption, injury or death.

The parallel is striking. Gospel ministry, once we take it outside, out of the relatively safe enclosure of a church building or a well-built pulpit and onto "the streets", is dangerous. All manner of pitfalls await us and without vigilance we become easy prey. The world is not a cozy place—or at least it should not be. Without even a hint of melodrama we can speak of gospel ministry as being frontline spiritual warfare.

That is how Paul sees it in the well-known passage on the armor of God in Ephesians 6 v 10-20. There are many treatments of this passage that ignore its gospel focus. As a result it is read as something fantastic, esoteric and maybe even a little bit spooky. Yet the gospel figures in v 15, where it is described as "the gospel of peace", and in v 17, where the sword of the Spirit is the word of God. And in v 19 Paul asks for prayer to make known "the mystery of the gospel" with boldness.

This means it is primarily when we get on with the task of gospel ministry that we find ourselves struggling not "against flesh and blood, but against the rulers, against the authorities, against the cosmic powers over this present darkness, against the spiritual forces of evil in the heavenly places" (6 v 12). Notice the emphatic repetition of the word "against" in order to convey the magnitude of the task. Is it any wonder that even Paul recognizes his need of prayerful support as he goes about his apostolic mission of taking the gospel to the Gentiles?

The size of the task and the scope of the opposition make this principle seem eminently reasonable: do not "go it alone". So this principle is a word of caution and restraint. But it also suggests a way forward.

Jesus sent His disciples out in pairs. And the church in Antioch, directed by the Holy Spirit, sent out Barnabas and Saul together. Throughout the second half of Acts there is a consistent picture of Paul working with colleagues. The imagery of Ephesians 6 is not of a solitary soldier, but of an army equipped and ready for battle. The whole context of Ephesians is the church. It is through the church, as a reconciled community, that "the manifold wisdom of God might now be made known to the rulers and authorities in the heavenly places" (3 v 10). The best way to take the gospel out is with your brothers and sisters. This is another way of looking at Principle No. 14: "A Christian community is a persuasive witness for the gospel." It is not simply a question of strength in numbers. It is the significance of Christian relationships. Seeing Christians relating to one another and loving each other is incredibly powerful. It is a means of authenticating the gospel. This functions not only when we meet together as church, but also when we work together in frontline gospel ministry.

Of course we should get out there and get on with it. But we must be careful. It is dangerous out there. There are temptations as well as opportunities, obstacles as well as openings. Getting out there together and getting on with it with the prayerful support and involvement of your church is surely the only way to go.

Questions for discussion

? What are the attractions of the "lone ranger" attitude? How does it reflect contemporary culture?

? The unbelieving world is a dangerous place, but separation is not an option. How are we to cope with this tension?

Ideas for action

What might this look like in practice? It could, for example, involve a couple of people getting involved in local politics. This would work if you had similar political convictions, or if you stood at different points on the political spectrum. You could work together in the same party or show uncommon respect and affection across the political divides. In a similar way, it could involve people getting jobs with the same company or joining the same local club or getting involved in the same community organization. For a time, a group from our church frequented the same pub together. Applying this principle has even meant members of the same church going to aerobics together. Are there areas of ministry in which you are currently engaged on your own? How could you get other people to share your vision?

10 PEOPLE ENABLED FOR SERVICE

Principle

Principle

Leaders provide an environment in which
people can flourish.

Consider this

James slipped into bed trying not to disturb his wife.
It was past midnight and she had gone to bed an hour
ago. He had had to finish his sermon and the notice sheet ready
for the meeting tomorrow. It had been another exhausting day:
sermon preparation, more of that endless admin, a meeting about
the church redecoration, a difficult pastoral visit, a quick visit to
the hospital, putting the kids to bed and then out to do the closing
talk at the youth meeting. And as sleep fell upon him, he felt guilty
for not having found time to pray. He did not mind the hard work—
though his wife was less happy about it. What was frustrating was
that there were so few people who were able or willing to do the
jobs he delegated to them.

Biblical background

Read Matthew 23 v 1-12

? How would you characterize the leadership style of the scribes and Pharisees?

? List their main deficiencies.

? In what ways are the disciples of Jesus to be different?

? Why are the titles of teacher, father and leader inappropriate?

Read all about it

Good leadership is vital. We see that again and again in the Old Testament. The quality of Israel's kings, prophets and priests had a major influence, often a decisive influence, on the state of the nation. And so, when we start to consider what good leadership involves, it is tempting to turn to the Old Testament. We have all heard sermons on "Nehemiah—the model leader".

But in the church Jesus—and not a human leader—is our prophet, priest and king. No longer do we have a leader who reveals the will of God (the prophet). Now Jesus reveals the Father to us through His word and Spirit. No longer do we have an intermediary who offers sacrifices on our behalf and intercedes for us (the priest). Now Jesus is our great high priest and the lamb who was slain. Through Him we each have access to the Father. No longer do we have someone ruling over us in God's place (the king). Now God Himself rules over each one of us through Christ, whom He has made Lord of all and Lord of the church.

It is Christ, and Christ alone, who rules the church. The leaders of a church do not rule over the church. There is only one person who rules the church and that is Christ. The most common model of leadership in the world, and one that is sadly all too common in the church, is specifically ruled out by Jesus. Christian leaders are not to lord it over others, to rule, to dominate (Mark 10 v 42; 1 Peter 5 v 3) or to seek pre-eminence (3 John 9-11). Elders are not lords, kings or rulers. That was one of the faults of the Pharisees (Matthew 23).

In 1 Timothy 3 v 3 Paul tells Timothy that elders must be "gentle"; that is, "mild, yielding, kind, forbearing". We need clear leadership and Christians are told to submit to their leaders, but such statements need to be set in a proper theological framework. Christ rules His church through His word and through His Spirit. The authority that leaders have is a mediated authority: they only exercise authority as they rightly teach and apply the word of God.

Is the alternative to dominant leadership some form of anarchy? Or should we be looking for humble, gentle leaders who will tell people what to do quietly and meekly? How can we have strong leadership that is not domineering? The answer is to find a new mental image of leadership—a more biblical image. Biblical leadership is not about inspiring or commanding people to follow you. It is to create an environment in which they can follow Christ their King. It is not about getting them to support your ministry, but about supporting the people of God in their ministries.

All believers are given gifts with which to serve God and build up the church. All are ministers. This is part of what it means to affirm the priesthood of all believers. There is not just one man who ministers in the church: all minister. "Minister" means simply "one who serves" and we have all been given gifts with which to serve one another and to serve God. The leaders, then, are those with the gifts of teaching and leadership (Romans 12 v 7-8), while others have different gifts (Romans 12 v 6-8; 1 Corinthians 12). And so leadership in the New Testament is not an office, it is a function. Leadership is not about the title you carry, it is what you do.

Leaders in the New Testament facilitate the ministries of all the other members. In Ephesians 4 v 11-13 Paul says that Christ has given some to be pastors and teachers "to equip the saints for the work of ministry, for building up the body of Christ, until we all attain to the unity of the faith and of the knowledge of the Son of God, to mature manhood, to the measure of the stature of the fullness of Christ". Building the church to maturity is achieved by "God's people", not by the pastors and teachers. The role of the leaders is to ensure that people's gifts and ministries are properly used and developed so that people work together for the building up of the church and extension of the kingdom of God.

Churches with a "one-man ministry" are unlikely to be very successful in training church leaders and church planters. There is not the space for people to grow and develop. And the jump to leadership is too great. We must learn to take risks with people and give them the space to fail.

Too often our desire is to be known as a church with good teaching. But good teaching, however engaging and orthodox, counts for nothing. What counts is good Bible learning and good Bible action. The measure of the teaching of our church is not the production of beautifully crafted sermons, but whether the word of God is preparing God's people for works of service.

Questions for discussion

? How does Christ lead His church?

? What do you think are the three things to which church leaders should devote most of their time?

? What is the difference between good Bible teaching and good Bible learning and action?

? What would it take for you to think of yourself as a minister of the gospel?

Ideas for action

Here are some suggestions for existing leaders:

- See the focus of your ministry as training and developing teachers and leaders who can lead and train others. Jealously guard time spent mentoring emerging leaders or key figures within the church.

- Encourage people to run with their own ideas rather than wait for you to come up with all the plans.

- Let people speak, lead meetings, and head up initiatives even if this means taking a few risks.

- Do not portray yourself as an invulnerable, flawless Christian—model "progress" rather than arrival (1 Timothy 4 v 15).

11 PEOPLE NOT PROGRAMS

Church activity is people-centered rather than
program-centered.

Consider this

Imagine a small church in Puddlemarsh. It has an
ageing congregation of good and godly people. It also
has a "Kids Klub", which has been running week in and week
out for years. There was a time when it was a thriving work and
reached many children and young people with the gospel, and
many became Christians as a result of it. Although it merits a
special place on the notice board, there really is no one with the
ability, energy or time to run it, and as a result it's in a state of
decline. Many in the church are troubled and asking what should
they do. There are those in the church who are too emotionally
attached to the club to allow it to stop. Yet the work is in danger of
falling into disrepute and the areas of ministry ideally suited to the
gifts of those now running it go neglected.

.rch

Biblical background

Read Romans 12 v 1-8

? How does Paul suggest we should determine our ministry?

? How should we use the gifts God has given us?

? What in this passage prevents an emphasis on using "my" gifts to justify individualism or indulgence?

Read all about it

Children. Singles. The homeless. Drug addicts. Senior citizens. Men. Women. The disabled. Young people. Single mums. Schools. Marrieds. Ethnic minorities. Debt counselling. The list is almost endless. They are all legitimate and important areas of ministry and a persuasive case could be argued for each one. But how do you choose?

It is at this point that reflection on God's providence is a great help in determining our activity. Jesus promised to build His church. In every local situation where the Lord is worshipped and His word obeyed, we can trust Him to be about that business. This means that the areas of gospel ministry a local church should be engaged in are those areas where there are members with the gifts and the heart to take responsibility for that ministry. That is what is meant by the phrase "gift-led".

This does not always happen. Church activity is often program-led with people found to service the program. This can mean that square pegs are driven into round holes. The result is that the ministry in question suffers, the individuals suffer and genuine gospel opportunities go begging. To make matters worse, the programs are likely to be the product of years of accumulation and tradition rather than a deliberate and relevant gospel strategy.

60

There are, for example, some people who are good at relating to the socially marginalised and there are some people who find it rather challenging. It just so happens that those who are good at relating in this way often enjoy doing so and those who are challenged in this area often find it tiresome and troublesome. Those who can relate and enjoy relating should be the ones who are encouraged, released, supported and resourced to get involved in relevant gospel ministry. A "round-pegs for round-holes" approach!

There is no need to get too hung up about precisely defining everyone's gifts. The lists of gifts in the New Testament are more about allowing people to be different and valuing that difference than they are about neatly pigeon-holing everyone. Let people pursue their passions. People are usually enthusiastic about what they are good at and they are usually good at what they are enthusiastic about.

However this can descend into an individualism in which we each get on with our own thing. Or it can justify an indulgence in which we only do what we feel comfortable doing. In Romans 12 and 1 Corinthians 12 Paul links gifts to the image of a body. Gifts are not exercised in isolation, but as part of a co-operating body. They are not given for self-indulgence, but to build up the church and its mission. Being part of a community where everything is done for the sake of the gospel is a dynamic environment. The gospel sets the agenda and everyone is involved in keeping it at the top of the agenda. Within such a context people will be thinking "gospel" and alert to needs and opportunities. As the church asks if it can respond, questions will be asked about resources and people. Individuals will be challenged to think if this particular ministry is for them. Identifying and developing gifts has an important corporate dimension. This is an area where godly leadership should be exercised—leadership that creates an environment in which the people of God can flourish and be all that God wants them to be.

So take a good look at your church program. More importantly take a look at your people. So much gospel ministry could be started if we were prepared to start with the people we have now rather than the program we had last year. So do not be afraid to stop something either—in gospel terms it could be the best thing you have done for years.

Questions for discussion

[?] Have you ever felt like a square peg in a round hole?

[?] Why do we find it so difficult to know what our gifts are?

[?] How can we help to develop one another's ministries?

Ideas for action

Take ten minutes to list your strengths. Ask someone else to list your strengths and compare the lists. Think about how your strengths relate to what you are currently doing and what you could potentially do. If everyone in your Bible-study group does this, you can talk through together whether there are new initiatives that some of you could begin.

Is there someone in your church who is a pain in the neck? They are just a little bit too enthusiastic; they have one too many good ideas; they are too ready to suggest areas of improvement. Instead of just putting up with them, why not think proactively about areas of ministry that they could pioneer?

12 PEOPLE NOT BUILDINGS

Principle

People are essential to a gospel ministry—
buildings are not.

Consider this

You have been approached by a church in Slovakia with whom your church has enjoyed a long-standing relationship. They want you to help them put up a church building in one of the nearby towns. You already help fund a young couple to work with teenagers and you periodically send money to help the church in its work among prostitutes. The money required for the building is about £100,000. They explain the need for it in terms of their church planting work, explaining that in their culture they are treated with suspicion if they don't have a place of worship. The question is going to be put before the church council this evening. How do you vote?

Biblical background

Read Ephesians 2 v 19-22

? In this section Paul talks about the household of God, a holy temple and the dwelling of God. To what is he referring?

? What was the significance of the temple in the Old Testament? How is that significance reflected in the new covenant "temple"?

? What are the foundations of this building? What is its cornerstone?

Read all about it

Where would we be without buildings? It is exceptionally difficult for many Christians to imagine church life without them. Where would we meet? How could we run our Friday lunch for senior citizens? What about the *Discovering Christianity* course? These are not easy questions to answer. The idea of being without a building is too much for some people to bear.

Consider youth work as a case in point. There are two meetings a week for young people between the ages of 14 and 18. The Sunday evening meeting takes place in a renovated room under the main church hall. It is spacious and youth friendly. There is an old TV with a games console, a pool table and a coffee bar with its own Espresso machine donated by one of the church members. It is clearly ideal for youth work. After the evening meeting the young people come down, make it their own and get taught the Bible. The Friday night event takes place in the main hall because it is a lot more boisterous with a closing Bible talk thrown in for good measure. All sorts of games are played—indoor hockey, basketball—although there are also quiet areas for listening to music and chilling out with friends.

It is hard to imagine successful youth work going on without a building. I am sure there are many people involved in youth work who hanker after the resources just described. Church buildings are so much part of our landscape and a key feature of the plans of many growing churches. This can be seen in the life-cycle of the new churches which grew out of the so-called house church movement of the early 'seventies. Many of them have graduated to "proper" buildings, some spending over £1 million for the privilege. But why shouldn't they? The received wisdom is so received that it is part of our ecclesiastical psyche. Everyone knows that dedicated buildings significantly increase what you can do for the church community and what you can offer to the wider community.

Yet the value or significance of buildings need not be argued on grounds of mere pragmatism—just ask the non-conformists of the nineteenth century. Walk down the high street of most British towns and you will see a non-conformist church building. As often as not it will be large and imposing. It may even boast some fine architecture. What is it saying? In essence it is saying that the non-established churches have become "establishment". They now enjoy "a place", a tangible presence, and therefore credibility, status and significance. They have arrived. They can no longer be dismissed as dissenting radicals on the fringes. They are part of the fabric of society—legitimate and recognized.

In some respects, this development revisited familiar territory. Church buildings did not start appearing on the landscape until well into the third century. It was only after the "conversion" of Constantine that the church started to have architectural aspirations. Church buildings arose out of a pagan context and their design reflected pagan temples. They expressed a desire on the part of church leaders to be seen as legitimate. Their splendor magnified as the status of the church increased. The development of buildings follows the movement of Christianity from outlawed sect to acceptable institution. And buildings still perform a similar function today—particularly if you can get the mayor to perform the official opening.

It is the same issue in an overseas context. Many churches that emerged out of communism immediately started building projects and were quick to ask Christians in the west to help them. Their buildings were necessary, we were told, because without them these churches would be regarded as cults. But what is new? That was the status of the New Testament churches. It did not seem to bother the apostles unduly nor hamper their evangelistic efforts.

But what is the point of this analysis? It highlights the difficulty we have with what at first sight seems so obvious: people are essential to gospel ministry while buildings are not. Everyone would assent to such a principle. Then why do we continue to pour money into buildings? Why do so many church plants start by looking for a building? Why are so many resources and so much time "invested" in bricks and mortar?

One evangelical church erected a fine edifice in the local community. But a number of years after the opening around £15,000 per month is still required to service the loans. How many hungry people would that sum feed? How many gospel projects would it fund? How many gospel workers would it resource in the UK and overseas?

This is not like Judas questioning the money spent on the perfume used to anoint Jesus. This is recognizing that church is the company of redeemed people. As Paul says in Ephesians 2, *we* are the living stones God is using for His holy temple. We are the ones who, through our lives individually and corporately, give credibility to the gospel. Buildings are at best tangential to that and at worst they may be a hindrance to it. It should be our ambition for people to be impressed by our lives, not our architecture.

This is not to suggest that every church should sell its building. But we should think seriously about our preoccupation with buildings. If you already have a building, try to develop the life of the church in ways that are not determined by it. If you do not have one, but think you need one, think again! One church was quoted £1.9 million to put in a balcony to meet the needs of their growing congregation. They chose to church plant instead. Adopt God's strategy: lives so transformed by the gospel that people see our good works and give glory to our Father in heaven.

Questions for discussion

- ❓ Why are people so often emotionally attached to their church building?

- ❓ Can you think of examples of where the building determines the strategy of the church rather than serving it?

- ❓ What are the advantages of holding meetings in homes or hired buildings?

Ideas for action

How much of your evangelism takes place within your building? Would some of this activity be more effective in other locations?

Some churches have chosen to build a community center instead of a "church" building. Are there ways in which you could make your building available for others to use during the week?

Next time refurbishment or extension of your building is discussed, ask the following questions:

- ❓ Could the money be better used employing or training a Christian worker?

- ❓ Are there better ways around the problem of an inadequate building, like church planting, hiring a hall or meeting in homes?

PART THREE

THE PRIORITY
OF COMMUNITY

13 THE PRIORITY OF COMMUNITY

Principle

The church is an extended family.

Consider this

A church meets at four o'clock on Sunday afternoons for an "open home". There are activities for the children in which some of the adults participate. But nothing is planned for the adults. They will reconvene at eight o'clock to study the Bible, pray together and discuss issues, but in the afternoon they simply mingle, chat and perhaps pray for one another. Is this an indulgent waste of time or does it model something important about church?

Biblical background

Read 1 Timothy 3 v 14-16

❓ In v 15 Paul talks about God's household or God's family. To what is he referring?

❓ Why did Paul write this letter to Timothy?

❓ What are the implications of the family model for relationships within the church (see 1 Timothy 5 v 1-2 and 6 v 1-2)?

❓ What are the implications of the family model for leadership within the church (see 1 Timothy 3 v 4-5)?

Read all about it

The word "family" is becoming popular on church notice boards as in "family church" and "family service". I am not entirely sure what these mean. I suspect that "family church" means you have a crèche and "family service" means that someone is going to be condescending to the children. Too cynical? Almost certainly. But I do think they suggest a notion of the church as a family that is a long way from that of the New Testament.

Families eat together, play together, cry together and laugh together. Families provide for one another. They share something of the task of bringing up children and they look after their older members (or at least they used to). Families do argue and fight, but they do not stop being families as a result—they have to find ways of working things out. And you cannot opt for another family just because it shares your taste in music or reading or whatever. Families do not buy special buildings to meet together. They might hire a hall for a special occasion, but most of the time you just have each other round. When you are with your family, you can take off your shoes and slump on the sofa. They provide identity and a place of belonging. Families define for us what is "home".

Now read that paragraph again substituting the word "church" for the word "family" and you will begin to get a sense of what Paul means when he calls the church "the family of God" in 1 Timothy 3 v 15. And you might also get a sense of how attractive church could be for a generation searching for identity and belonging.

The Gospels make it clear that the church family has a greater claim on us than our biological families (Matthew 10 v 34-37 and Mark 3 v 31-35). But our domesticated religion tempers this bold assertion. Discussing Christian service, we say: "Obviously, you need to put your family first". The word "obviously" is revealing. Lacking biblical justification, we turn instead to what is "obvious" according to the standards of our culture. While the church should support the family as a God-ordained institution, we do not give it our ultimate allegiance. Is it too much to suggest that for some Christians their biological family has become an idol?

The church as a family builds on the salvation-language of new birth and adoption. Conversion sometimes means leaving one family. It always means joining a new one.

Perhaps the problem is our image of the ideal family: father, mother, 2.4 children, mortgage and a reliable car. Complete, self-contained and—all too often—self-absorbed. The problem with "family first" comes when our notion of family is too narrow. Families in Israel were very different. They spanned generations and they included slaves. They offered immigrants a place of belonging. And their boundaries were blurred: clan, tribe, even the nation itself could be viewed as a family. And that is what church is to be like: inter-generational and inclusive; a place of belonging and identity; both local and global.

People's experience of family varies considerably. Thankfully for many their family has nurtured and cared for them. In their families they have learnt respect, tolerance and debate. They have learned to be both free individuals and part of a community of relationships in which the individual is not sovereign. Thomas Manton, in a letter which accompanied the documents of the 17th-century Westminster Assembly, described the family as "the seminary of the church and commonwealth".

But other people's experience of family has been more mixed and in some cases tragic. Some have experienced family as repressive and stifling; for others it has meant abuse and danger. Yet the very experience of pain reflects the human need for a place of care and belonging. One single mother enjoyed coming to church for the simple reason that it was the first time she had met men who were not cruel.

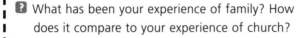

Questions for discussion

❓ What has been your experience of family? How does it compare to your experience of church?

❓ "Is it too much to suggest that for some Christians their biological family has become an idol?"

❓ How would you summarize Jesus' teaching on family (read Matthew 10 v 34-37 and Mark 3 v 31-35)?

Ideas for action

How can you let family start to define church? The simplest thing you can do is to include single people in your family life. In one church a number of families have single people round one evening each week for a meal—and that includes 20-year-old singles and 80-year-old widows. Offer your home as a place where singles can entertain their friends—and see Christian family in action at the same time. Families are where most people turn in times of need. But what about those from dysfunctional families? You could look after a single parent's children for the day, giving the parent some time to themselves.

Or how about this? Start playing around with this principle: "If you wouldn't do it in a family, then you shouldn't do it as a church." It does not always work. Families do not submerge members under water and they do not recruit new members—although good families are welcoming and inclusive. But give it a try and see where it takes you. Then have a go with: "If you do it in a family, then you can do it as a church".

14 A PERSUASIVE COMMUNITY

Principle

A Christian community is a persuasive witness for the gospel.

Consider this

Your Bible-study group has decided to have a trip to the cinema, a country walk and a barbeque every fortnight over the next six weeks. But then you discover that your church has planned a six-week *Discovering Christianity* course over the same period. You were going to invite some of your friends from work to the Bible-study group socials. Now the pressure is on to get them to the course. "Why spend your time just having a good time," you are told by one of your church leaders, "when you could be inviting them to an evangelistic event?" It is hard to say "No" to evangelism, but you are uneasy. You would love friends to do an evangelistic course, but you doubt whether they would come at this point in time. You think having them meet your Christian friends could be the best way forward, but is that just a cop out? And then there is Mary. A course would be way over her head and yet she seems to love being with Christians.

Biblical background
Read John 17 v 20-23

❓ Who are the people for whom Jesus is praying (v 20)?

❓ What does He ask for them in v 21 and why does He ask it?

❓ What are the two consequences of unity in v 23?

❓ In what ways can Christians show this unity?

Read all about it

People today are cynical. They have seen too many adverts. They no longer trust those who proclaim the truth. They suspect all claims to know the truth are driven by power and money. If a scientist says GM foods are safe, they assume he or she is in the pay of industry. And if a preacher proclaims the only way to God, they dismiss it as self-serving arrogance. The greatest crime of our age (sometimes, it seems, the only crime) is intolerance. But while people may not be seeking the truth, they *do* crave authenticity. And while they may not be looking for a worldview, they do long for identity and belonging.

Now imagine a story of a king who laid aside his power and came in weakness and humility; a king who said that true authority was exercised through service; a king despised by the powerful and welcomed by the marginalised; a king who gave his life to set his subjects free. What a potent truth that would be in our generation.

And imagine a community of people who offered identity and belonging; a community committed to a truth that was liberating; a community with leaders who saw themselves as servants; a community who put the truth it believed into practice through the service of others; a community that not only acknowledged its failures, but wove them into the fabric of its story. What a powerful witness that would be. What a powerful defense of the gospel message.

Jesus said: "A new commandment I give to you, that you love one another: just as I have loved you, you also are to love one another. By this all people will know that you are my disciples, if you have love for one another" (John 13 v 34-35).

Christian community is a vital part of Christian mission. Mission takes place as people see our love for one another. We all know that the gospel is communicated both through the words we say and the lives we live. What Jesus says is that it is the life we live together that counts. The life of the Christian community is part of the way by which the gospel is communicated. Lesslie Newbigin describes the local congregation as "the hermeneutic of the gospel"—the way in which people understand the gospel.

We need to be communities of love. And we need to be seen to be communities of love. People need to encounter the church as a network of relationships rather than a meeting you attend or a place you enter. Mission must involve not only contact between unbelievers and individual Christians, but between unbelievers and the Christian community.

In my experience of church planting, time after time people have been attracted to the Christian community *before* they were attracted to the Christian message. Of course attraction to the Christian community is not enough. The gospel is a word. Conversion involves believing the truth. But our generation—and perhaps there is nothing special about them in this—understands the gospel message better when it is set in the context of a gospel community.

Every "text" has a "context". This is an important principle of Bible interpretation. But it is as true of mission. Every time you communicate the message of the gospel you do so in a context. And that context affects the meaning that people give to your message. If you talk about God's grace while constantly condemning other people's lifestyles, then you should not be surprised if you are misunderstood. Nor will you be understood if you talk about God's love, while you exhibit bitterness and envy. According to Jesus, the best context for gospel communication is a distinctive, caring, inclusive Christian community. It is important that your unbelieving friends meet your believing friends so they can see how you relate to one another.

Most mission strategies involve two elements:

- Building relationships

- Sharing the gospel message

But if the believing community is vital for a persuasive witness, then we should add a third element:

- Including people in community

It is not enough to build a relationship between one believer and one unbeliever. We need to introduce people to the network of relationships that make up that believing community so that they see Christian community in action.

Our modern worldview was built upon the assertion that truth was determined by autonomous human reason, fashioning us in the process into autonomous human individuals. But things have developed so that now we have all become creators of our own truth. The issue is no longer whether something is true, but whether it is true for me.

But we are not autonomous. God said: "Let *us* make man in *our* image." (Genesis 1 v 26). We were created as beings-in-relationship. And so people sit alone or in their self-contained families watching the American sitcom *Friends*—enjoying at a distance the community for which we were made. It does not require a great leap of imagination to realize that church as extended family is not simply a biblical norm or a great context for discipleship—though it is both those things; it is also a powerful gospel testimony.

Ideas for action
Thinking about the three elements of gospel work enables us to work out mission through community in practical ways.

⮟ Building relationships with people

⮟ Sharing the gospel message

⮟ Including people in community

Think about the people you are trying to reach with the gospel or would like to start reaching. Identify ideas—often very ordinary ideas—for building relationships with them, sharing the gospel message and introducing them to the network of believing relationships. Those introductions might involve nothing more sophisticated than inviting both Christian and non-Christian friends for a meal or for an evening out. Or it might mean including non-Christians on a church outing.

Gospel-centered church

15 A WELCOMING COMMUNITY

Principle

People need to understand what is happening
in Christian meetings.

Consider this

Sarah had been a member of Washwood Evangelical
Church for about two years. There was much about it
that she really enjoyed and benefited from. She had really grown
since she had become a Christian and she knew for a fact that her
conversion had encouraged everyone in the church. But she just
could not bring herself to invite any of her non-Christian friends
along to the meetings. She had tried once, and her mates said they
liked the people, but they thought some of the things that went
on were just weird. "Why do they talk like that when they pray?",
they had asked her. "What on earth is this obsession with the blood
of the lamb?" they enquired, "and what on earth is an Ebenezer?"
Sarah tried to explain, but she did not know all the answers either.
Sometimes she was as confused as they were. It was such a shame
because Simon was such a good preacher. Apart from when he kept
talking about propiti-something or other, that is.

Biblical background
Read 1 Corinthians 14 v 20-25

- In what ways were the Corinthian Christians being immature (v 20)?
- Why might an unbeliever accuse the church of being crazy (v 23)?
- What convicts the unbeliever in v 24?
- What is the result of this conviction?

Read all about it

1 Corinthians 12 – 14 is an important passage about what happens when the church meets together. It has more to say about our attitude than it does about our practice—the need for us to be concerned about other people in the congregation, be they Christians or non-Christians.

Paul begins by dealing in 12 v 1 with the question of what it means to be "spiritual"—and the use of the gifts were primarily an example of how the faulty spirituality of some within the church of Corinth expressed itself. They were preoccupied with themselves and exercised the various manifestations of the Spirit—particularly tongues—in order to demonstrate their lofty attainments and status. Paul debunks the very idea of a two-tier Christianity. Even the most basic of all Christian confessions, "Jesus is Lord", can only be truly spoken through the enabling of the Holy Spirit (12 v 3). Paul then deals with the issue of gifts given by the Spirit "for the common good".

The gifts are then graded on the basis of their usefulness to the whole congregation. The desire to be spiritual was a godly desire (14 v 1), but true spirituality expresses itself in a commitment to the good of others; in an eagerness to see them encouraged and edified. Hence the "priority" of prophecy over tongues (14 v 4). What follows is teaching on the necessity of the mind in the whole edification process. For believers to be built up in the faith in the congregation, truth must be spoken and understood. The mind has to be active and fruitful (14 v 14) because if the mind is not actively involved in apprehending truth, there can be no growth in godliness.

According to Paul, this principle also operates when non-Christians are present among the congregation (14 v 20-25). The mind of unbelievers have to be addressed—phenomena are not enough. In fact, if the phenomenon in question is the unregulated use of tongues, as was the case in Corinth, then it actually prevents non-Christians from coming to faith because it functions as a sign of God's judgment. It unnecessarily drives them away because they have not been able to understand. Whereas prophecy, because it is intelligible speech, can serve as that which brings the unbelievers to their senses, causing them to acknowledge God's presence among His people.

There are a number of issues raised by these chapters. I will mention just three:

- Intelligibility is essential when the church meets.
- Our contribution should aim at helping others.
- The presence of non-Christians should influence our practice.

Martin Luther, despite the presence of academics in his congregation, claimed that he always preached so as to be understood by the servant girls who were there. Such a desire to communicate the truths of the gospel to as many people as possible is surely a mark of true godliness. This requires us to think about what we do when we meet and why we are doing it. It influences the language we use in our songs and in our sermons.

Church meetings are increasingly alien environments for many non-Christians. Yet it is right and appropriate to invite our non-Christian friends into our meetings, even if their status is that of observers. From that position they will be able to see the commitment of Christians to one another. They will hear as we acknowledge the greatness of God. They will be able to listen to the word of God being taught in all of its contemporary relevance and power. To facilitate this we need to take the time and trouble to explain what we are doing and why we are doing it. Ritual may impress unbelievers, but it will not convert them. Only the truth of the gospel will do that. This is as basic as explaining why we sing as well as what we sing. It means talking people through communion and using a baptismal service—whatever the mode and whoever the recipient—as an opportunity for communicating the gospel by explaining the procedure. We need to take time to explain prayer in terms of both "the what" and "the why". If all of these activities arise out of the gospel—as they do—they are all tremendous opportunities for the gospel. _exvalesm_

This is not "seeker friendly," but it is non-Christian sensitive. This means that we do not need to change our church meetings to

something can be done by or in church

rebecca
plans

maria/
rachel

getting use
to quarter

Brittney
heart condition
and more hope

Wendy

Savannah
Jackson

better way on
best friend
v/ God

a presentational style in order to reach unbelievers. Potentially at least, there is something inherently evangelistic about Christians meeting to encourage each other and provoke one another to godliness. A recent study showed that the majority of non-Christians are converted not so much through our special evangelistic events, where they know they are being targeted, but through attending "ordinary" church meetings in which they observe Christians taking the gospel seriously.

But if we are to encourage each other to bring non-Christians along, we need to be aware of the "cringe factor" and of the many cultural hurdles we inadvertently erect through our insensitivity. In the final analysis, this is not a question of technique, approach, style or preference. It is about passion: a passion for those who are without God and therefore without hope in the world.

Questions for discussion

? Why should we invite non-Christians to our meetings?

? Do you hesitate to invite your non-Christians friends to church? Why is this?

? Paul says the Corinthians' use of tongues was egocentric. In what ways might contemporary Christian spirituality share this danger?

? What is the difference between being seeker-friendly and non-Christian sensitive?

Ideas for action

⊟ If you teach in the church from time to time, ask a twelve-year-old to read or listen to your sermon or Bible study before you "deliver" it.

⊟ If you choose the songs and hymns for a meeting, explain their meaning and language. As a group, choose a few of the popular songs sung in your church and explain them to one another.

⊟ Write out a 90-second explanation of communion, prayer, the Bible and baptism that could be used by someone leading a meeting.

16 AN INCLUSIVE COMMUNITY

Principle

People will be more willing to respond to the gospel
if they have a sense of belonging before they feel the
necessity to believe.

Consider this

Nick is not interested in Jesus. But he is interested in
playing the drums. Nick would love to play drums in the
music group of your church, which his wife, Barbara, attends. He
does not mind that they are Christian songs—he does not have to
sing them and he can slip out for a smoke during the sermon.

At least Nick will not be disruptive. Not like George. His mind is
slightly addled. He sings enthusiastically, though not necessarily
when everyone else does. And he has a tendency to heckle during
the sermon. It was endearing the first time, but has now gone
beyond a joke. And another thing: he smells. No one is going to
turn him away, but then neither is anyone going to invite him over
for Sunday lunch.

Biblical background
Read Luke 5 v 27-32 and 19 v 1-10

❓ What was the significance of eating with people that
made the on-lookers so scandalized by Jesus' behavior
in these two incidents (5 v 30 and 19 v 7)?

❓ In the case of Zacchaeus, which came first: a changed life or
inclusion by Jesus?

❓ What is the link between the inclusivity of Jesus' meal tables
and the nature of the gospel (5 v 31-32 and 19 v 9-10)?

Read all about it

Have you ever wondered why it is that the tax-collectors and prostitutes were so attracted to Jesus and yet the church does not seem to attract such people today? Or to put it another way: why is it that when Paul says God chooses the weak, foolish and lowly people to shame the powerful, wise and noble (1 Corinthians 1 v 26-31), British churches are full of bright middle-class people, and we have a whole industry built around "celebrity" Christians?

inclusive welcoming

I am not sure I know the answer, but I do know that Jesus went out of His way to include the marginalised and sinners. And the religious people of His day scorned Him for it. The religious people wanted nothing to do with such people. But Jesus was accused of being a glutton and a drunkard, a friend of tax collectors and sinners (Matthew 11 v 19).

does not judge

kind love

Consider the setting of the parables of the lost sheep, the lost coin and the lost son in Luke 15:

> Now the tax collectors and sinners were all drawing near to hear him. And the Pharisees and the scribes grumbled, saying, "This man receives sinners and eats with them." (Luke 15 v 1-2)

knows who he is in the Lord

Jesus welcomed sinners. He included them. He let them tag along. He gave them a sense of belonging. And He ate with them—the supreme sign in the culture of His day of belonging and inclusion. They were His friends. They were part of His community.

The parables of the lost sheep and the lost coin vindicate Jesus' approach. God's Messiah has come for the lost. The parable of the lost son (and which son is it that is lost?) adds a twist. The Pharisees were like the elder son. They would not mingle with the sinners and so they risked being left outside the party.

grace

Perhaps the key thing is that Jesus modeled the gospel in the welcome He gave to people and in His willingness to eat with them. In so doing He embodied the grace of God. Who do you welcome to your meal table? People with good manners, clean finger nails and bright conversation? Who do you welcome into the membership of your church? People of good standing with respectable lives?

We come to Christ with nothing. Only through the power of the gospel can we begin to sort out the mess we have made of our lives. We all know that. So we need to ask whether in practice we expect people's behavior to change before they can be part of our community. We can too easily preach salvation by grace, but model salvation by works.

It can very subtle. I remember being in a Bible-study group where someone was vehemently asserting that in our church we did not erect barriers to belonging. Meanwhile, on the same night in another Bible-study group, a new Christian was talking about how he felt there were a number of hoops he had to jump through before he really felt as if he belonged in our church.

A minister in Scotland was once standing outside his church when a drunk walked past. "Why don't you come in?" he asked. "I will," said the drunk, "when I get my life sorted out". The minister was quick-witted enough to question whether this was likely. But he was left with a more fundamental question: "Whoever gave him the impression that church was for people who had got their lives sorted out?" And the answer, of course, is that we have.

We have already noted in this book how time after time people are attracted to the Christian community before they are attracted to the Christian message. The best place for belief to emerge is in a context where people already feel they belong. If a believing community is a persuasive witness for the gospel (see Principle 14), then people need to be included to see that witness at work. The best way to draw people in is not to make them feel on the outside of what is going on, but to include and involve them.

I remember a woman with an alcoholic husband and two disruptive children. What she liked about coming to our church was that we did not show disapproval when her children misbehaved. We welcomed her and her children along with the disruption they brought. It was decisive in her Christian experience. In the case of another woman, an elderly widow, there is little doubt that she initially got involved with our church because she was lonely. Church meant people who would talk to her, people who would visit her, somewhere to go. But as a result she was converted and is now one of the most gracious and godly Christian women I know.

Treat people as part of the church even before, in a sense, they really are. It will get messy at times. Church life is a lot easier if you only let respectable, sorted-out people into the church in the first place. Other churches may raise their eyebrows. But drunkard, glutton, friend of sinners—these should be badges of honor among those who follow Jesus Christ. *what is your def. of honor?*

Questions for discussion

❓ Why are most western churches generally failing to reach working-class people with the gospel?

❓ "We can too easily preach salvation by grace, but model salvation by works." Can you identify any evidence for this statement?

❓ What might be the contemporary equivalent of the accusation that Jesus was "a glutton and a drunkard, a friend of tax collectors and sinners" (Matthew 11 v 19)?

Ideas for action

People on the fringe of your church will not be able to preach sermons or lead in prayer. But they can wash up, set up a computer, play in the football team, decorate the church hall. Involve people by asking them to do something.

Ask recent converts what were the hurdles they felt they had to jump to be part of your church community. Which of these reflect the gospel and which reflect your sub-culture?

17 A MULTIPLYING COMMUNITY

Principle

Local churches grow by starting new churches.

Consider this

Simon is the leader a church of almost 100 people. "That's not bad," he tells himself. "It's more than most local ministers have in their churches." But now one of the Bible-study groups has come up with a plan to start a new church in a new housing estate. Simon's not opposed to this idea—well, not exactly. He's just worried that they will be spreading their resources too thinly. One of the likely new leaders is currently a prime mover in the youth work. Another potential leader heads up the music group. Truth be told, Simon is not sure he wants to be the leader of a church of 60 again. Yet something nags at his conscience. Who will reach the new housing estate, or the rough area on the other side of town, or the thousands of other people in the town who never get to hear the gospel?

Biblical background
Read Romans 16 v 3-5 and 10-11

❓ Where did the congregations in Rome meet?

❓ What do you think happened as congregations grew?

❓ How does meeting in a smaller group safeguard the biblical principles of (a) mutual care and discipleship; (b) participation and inclusion; and (c) a focus on mission rather than maintenance?

Read all about it

Contemporary empirical evidence suggests that it is denominations with a commitment to church planting that are growing. Statistics show that small congregations grow proportionally faster than large congregations. A study by Christian Schwarz called *Natural Church Development* found that churches of 1-100 members had seen 32 new people over a five-year period while churches of 300-400 had seen only 25. These are good, pragmatic reasons for church planting. But this chapter focuses on the *biblical* reasons for church planting.

Principle 1 reminded us that mission is at the heart of the church: "mission is the central purpose of the church in the world". This principle reminds us that the church is at the heart of mission. At the center of God's plan of salvation are a family and a nation. God's purposes are not focused on many unrelated individuals, but upon His people. And God's purposes are not only to redeem a people for Himself, but also to reconcile them with one another. God's great plan of reconciliation is realized in the church.

And so the church is the focus of God's saving purposes. If the individual is at the heart of God's purposes, then it is quite natural to put the individual at the heart of mission—and many people do that. But if the church is at the heart of God's purposes and of Christ's saving work, we need not be embarrassed about making it the heart of mission.

In John 13 Jesus says: "A new commandment I give to you, that you love one another: just as I have loved you, you also are to love one another. By this all people will know that you are my disciples, if you have love for one another" (John 13 v 34-35; see also John 17 v 23). Christian community is an important part of Christian mission. Mission takes place as people see our love for one another. Principle 14 says: "A Christian community is a persuasive witness for the gospel".

We all know that the gospel is communicated both through the words we say and the lives we live. What Jesus says is that it is the life we live together that counts. The life of the Christian *more that this mission from God is not to be done alone. (church is a body)*

community is part of the way by which the gospel is communicated. And so mission cannot be done by a lone ranger. Mission must be done by a community of believers. Mission cannot be done in hit-and-run raids. There must be a community that can be observed and that offers a place of belonging. When we think "mission", we must think "church". And the best way to link church and mission is through church planting.

And so it is no surprise to find that for Paul mission meant planting churches. In the New Testament, wherever the gospel was preached, local churches were established. Luke portrays Paul as a church planter with a church planting team. The team functions as a church even as a church grows up around it, providing a context for discipleship and a demonstration of Christian community. In fact, at the beginning of 1 Corinthians 9 Paul defines his apostle-ship both in terms of his vision of the risen Christ and his work as a church planter. Apostolic mission was church planting.

Not only did Paul plant churches, but he planted reproducing churches. Church planting was part of normal New Testament church life. The apostolic churches were networks of self-repli-cating household churches that would continue Paul's mission by being missionary churches. Church planting was built into their nature. Paul planted churches as a bridgehead into a city. They would reach that city by continually replicating themselves.

Constantly replicating churches was the pattern of apostolic mission, but it was a pattern that gave fullest expression to the principles of Christian community. The New Testament pattern of church life implies a regular planting of new churches because:

- church planting creates space in which new leaders can emerge.

- church planting enables the fullest possible expression of New Testament "one anothering". Teaching one another, exhorting one another, discipling one another, caring for one another, praying with one another—all of these flourish best in the family atmosphere of a small group.

⬇ church planting creates a simplicity that prevents a maintenance mentality—there are no expensive buildings to maintain or complex programs to run.

⬇ church planting determines a style that is participatory and inclusive—just like Jesus' approach to discipleship and evangelism. The grace of God is powerfully embodied around an inclusive meal table as it was in Jesus' ministry.

⬇ the priesthood of all believers finds fullest expression when nobody's contribution gets lost in the crowd.

This has profound implications for our view of church growth. People resist church planting because they do not want to leave a large group for a small group. Large churches shape our image of success. We all want to be like large churches with full-time staff, music group, youth and children's work, building, office, notice sheets and so on. And so we hesitate to release people and resources. But the church in the New Testament chose to grow by dividing and reproducing, not by building larger auditoriums. A vision for church growth must be a vision for church planting.

Above all, church planting puts the gospel right back at the heart of church life. Let us be honest: we all drift towards comfort and complacency. The maintenance of church life too easily overwhelms an evangelistic cutting edge. Church planting means both the new churches and the sending church must start afresh with the gospel at the center. Church planting means the church lives very consciously in a missionary situation. That is what makes church planting so exciting.

Questions for discussion

- ❓ What are the main biblical reasons for church planting?

- ❓ What are the common reasons why churches do not plant other churches? How legitimate are they?

- ❓ What are the advantages of a small, new congregation over a large, well-established congregation? What are the disadvantages?

Ideas for action

For practical guidance on the process of church planting, see also "further reading" on page 96.

But if church planting seems too big a step at present, why not re-style your Bible-study group as a missionary community? Think through with your Bible-study group the characteristics of your neighborhood or focus on a community of people who you want to reach. Think about how you might build relationships with them, create opportunities to share the gospel and introduce them to others in the Bible-study group. Plan some evangelistic events as a group. Start praying together for your evangelistic strategy. Colin Marshall's book, *The Growth Group Manual* (Matthias Media / The Good Book Co., 1995), provides great practical help on leading a small group and making it focused on gospel growth.

A church in Leicester, England has begun a similar process. The leader selected one Bible-study group and re-styled it as "little church" with the message: "Everything that church is—you are". Teaching, praise, developing gifts, pastoral care and outreach were all now the responsibility of "little church" just as much as the Sunday gathering of "big church". There was some suspicion at first, but calling it a prototype helped to diffuse much of the opposition. Now that people have had a chance to see how it works, the other groups cannot wait to do the same.

Gospel-centered church

CONCLUSION:
IT'S ALL ABOUT THE GOSPEL

Principle

All church structures and activities should be evaluated by how they help the spread of the gospel.

 Biblical background

Read 1 Corinthians 9 v 19-23

▸ Why does Paul make himself "a servant to all" (v 19)?

▸ How can a Jew like Paul speak about "becoming" a Jew?

▸ What might it have meant for Paul to become "as one outside the law" (v 21)?

▸ Why is Paul's becoming "all things to all people" (v 22) different from "pleasing all the people all the time"?

▸ Is Paul's boast of doing everything for the sake of the gospel in v 23 peculiar to him because he was an apostle (see 1 Corinthians 11 v 1)?

 Read all about it

Church programs can be very intimidating. They can actually determine the kind of church we are rather than be the outworking of the kind of church we want to be. The majority of our churches have a history, as well, and with history comes tradition and with tradition often comes a rule of law. An interesting exercise on your way to work is to look at the notice boards of the church buildings you pass. Many of them have the weekly list of activities printed in gold lettering. The message is: in a world of change, this is where you will find stability. The church is there and on any given day of the week you can know what is going on come rain or shine.

This final principle of gospel ministry is a mandate for change and on-going change. It is about putting everything under the spotlight of the gospel and asking a simple question: how does this help get the gospel out to the world?

By now you may be nurturing a suspicion about these principles of gospel ministry. You may suspect that we have been passing off as profound or radical or fresh what are in fact statements of the obvious. What can we say in response? We hope you are right. These gospel principles must surely be bread-and-butter stuff to gospel people. "Of course, of course," I hear you say as you read them. The best we can hope for is the odd: "Well put".

But the fun starts when you begin stating the negative implications of these gospel principles. If we believe this, then we will not do that.

- If mission is the defining purpose of the church, then we will not make mission one activity among many.

- If the church is defined by the gospel and mutual commitment, then we will not clutter up the practice of church with constitutions, offices, buildings and so on.

- If the church is a family, then we will not make it a well-oiled organization.

- If a believing community is a vital witness for the gospel, then we will not reduce church to attendance at a meeting.

- If effective gospel ministry is long-term, low-key and relational, then we will not organize national evangelistic campaigns in sports stadia.

- If worship is a life-thing, then we will not put our energies into beautifully polished music.

- If the greatest error is not taking gospel initiatives, then we will not avoid taking risks.

☲ If leadership is about facilitating others and church activity is gift-led, then we will not make people fit into our plans or programs.

☲ If church planting is on the agenda, then we will not grow into a large congregation.

☲ If people are more important than buildings, then we will not put our money into buildings.

I can already hear the qualifications flooding in. But it is those qualifications that account for the gap between our practice and principles.

The assumption behind this principle is that the church exists because of the gospel and for the gospel. It is the gospel that gave her birth and it is for the gospel that she lives. Which means that we have come full circle: this final principle is the logical conclusion of the first, that "mission is the central purpose of the church in the world".

This last principle is, in effect, a summary principle. This is the test that we should be applying to all our activities as Christians and churches, whether that is mission, worship, leadership, nurture, gatherings and so on. This is the test of being an "evangelical"—a gospel person.

FURTHER READING

Tim Chester and Steve Timmis, **Total Church** (IVP/Crossway, 2006/2008)—looks at how every area of the Christian life should be gospel-centered and community-centered.

Tim Chester and Steve Timmis, **The World We All Want: A Course on How the Bible Really Works** (The Good Book Company, 2011)—a seven-session evangelistic Bible overview which keeps the church central to the gospel story.

The Crowded House:
www.thecrowdedhouse.org
The Porterbrook Network:
www.theporterbrooknetwork.org

Gospel-centered life
Becoming The Person God Wants You To Be

Sympathetic to our struggles... clear and concise... rooted in the Bible... relevant to our everyday experience... The Gospel-Centred Life shows how every Christian can follow the way of the cross as they embrace the liberating grace of God in Christ.

Gospel-centered marriage
Becoming The Couple God Wants You To Be

To understand why marriages struggle—as they all do—we need to understand the nature of our sin. To make marriages work, we need to understand how to apply the truth about God and His salvation. This study guide on Christian marriage focuses on how the Gospel shapes the practical realities of everyday life. Tim Chester lifts the lid on many of the common pressure points, and shows how a proper understanding of the Gospel can shape a response.

Gospel-centered family
Becoming The Parents God Wants You To Be

Many books aim to raise up competent, balanced parents and well-trained, well-rounded children. But Tim Chester and Ed Moll focus on families growing God-knowing, Christ-confessing, grace-receiving, servant-hearted, mission-minded believers – adults and children together. In twelve concise chapters, it challenges us to become the distinctively different people that God, through His gospel, calls us to be.

Gospel-centered leadership
Becoming The Servant God Wants You To Be (Published Summer 2012)

Steve Timmis shares his wealth of experience and understanding in church leadership of all kinds, and strips away the modern management and marketing techniques to get back to basics. How does the gospel determine the shape, priorities and content of our leadership? Vital reading for anyone in local-church leadership of any kind.

FOR MORE INFORMATION AND TO ORDER:
www.thegoodbook.com
Tel: 866 244 2165 email: sales@thegoodbook.com